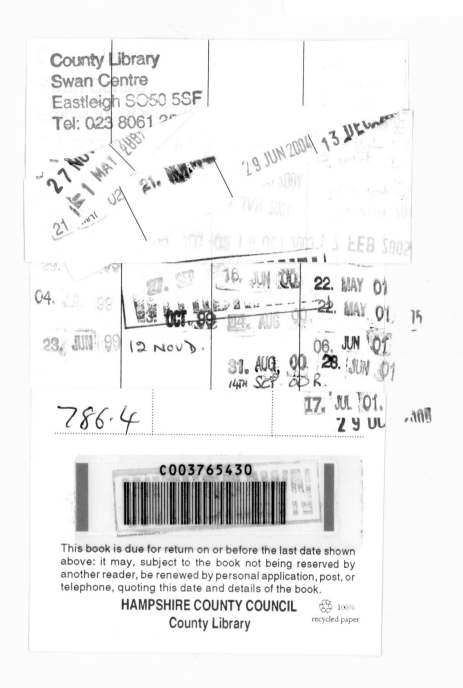

EASIEST
KEYBOARD
COLLECTION

WEST

Film Themes

WISE PUBLICATIONS
London/New York/Paris/Sydney/Copenhagen/Madrid

Exclusive Distributors:

Music Sales Limited
8/9 Frith Street,
London W1V 5TZ, England.

Music Sales Pty Limited
120 Rothschild Avenue,
Rosebery, NSW 2018,
Australia.

Order No. AM952050
ISBN 0-7119-7137-4
This book © Copyright 1998 by Wise Publications

Book design by Chloë Alexander
Compiled by Peter Evans
Music arranged by Derek Jones
Music processed by Paul Ewers Music Design

Printed in the United Kingdom by
Caligraving Limited, Thetford, Norfolk.

Photographs courtesy of:
Image Bank

Your Guarantee of Quality
As publishers, we strive to produce every book to the highest
commercial standards.
The music has been freshly engraved and the book has been carefully
designed to minimise awkward page turns and to make playing from
it a real pleasure.
Particular care has been given to specifying acid-free, neutral-sized
paper made from pulps which have not been elemental chlorine
bleached. This pulp is from farmed sustainable forests and was
produced with special regard for the environment.
Throughout, the printing and binding have been planned to ensure
a sturdy, attractive publication which should give years of enjoyment.
If your copy fails to meet our high standards, please inform us and
we will gladly replace it.

Music Sales' complete catalogue describes thousands of titles and is
available in full colour sections by subject, direct from Music Sales
Limited. Please state your areas of interest and send a cheque/postal
order for £1.50 for postage to: Music Sales Limited, Newmarket Road,
Bury St. Edmunds, Suffolk IP33 3YB.

Visit the Internet Music Shop at
http://www.musicsales.co.uk

Contents

A WHOLE NEW WORLD
(From Walt Disney Pictures' "Aladdin")

Music by Alan Menken. Lyrics by Tim Rice

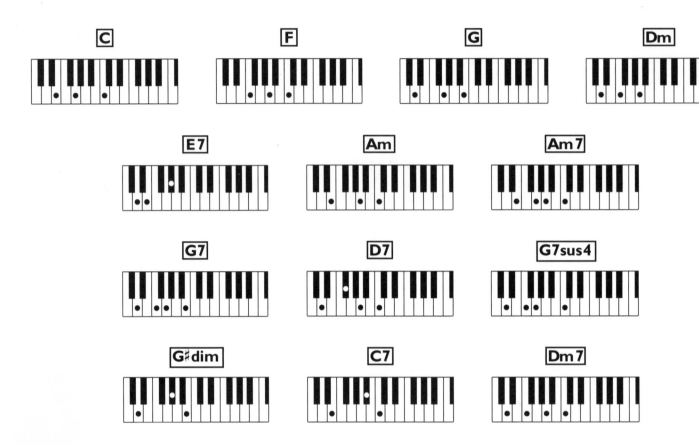

Voice:	**Horn**
Rhythm:	**16 beat**
Tempo:	♩ = 100

I can show— you the world   shin - ing, shim - mer - ing,   splen - did.

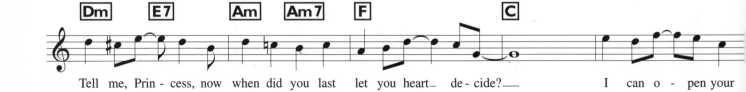

Tell me, Prin - cess, now when did you last   let you heart— de - cide?—   I can o - pen your

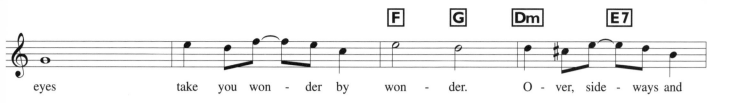

eyes   take   you   won - der   by   won - der.   O - ver, side - ways and

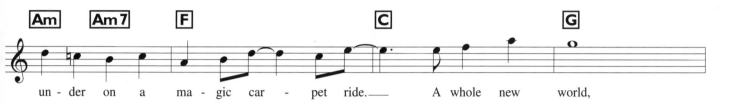

un - der   on   a   ma - gic   car - pet   ride.___   A   whole   new   world,

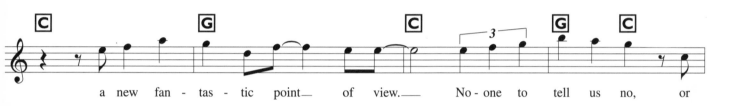

a   new   fan - tas - tic   point___   of   view.___   No - one   to   tell   us   no,   or

where   to   go   or   say   we're   on - ly   dream - ing.   A   whole   new   world,

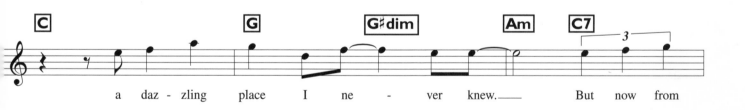

a   daz - zling   place   I   ne - ver   knew.___   But   now   from

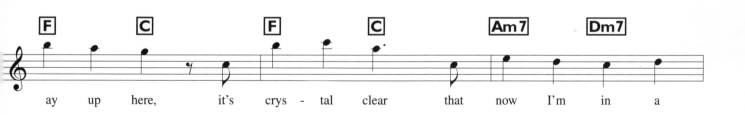

ay   up   here,   it's   crys - tal   clear   that   now   I'm   in   a

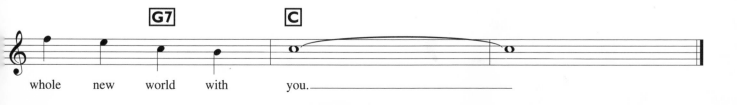

whole   new   world   with   you.___

ALFIE

Music by Burt Bacharach
Lyric by Hal David

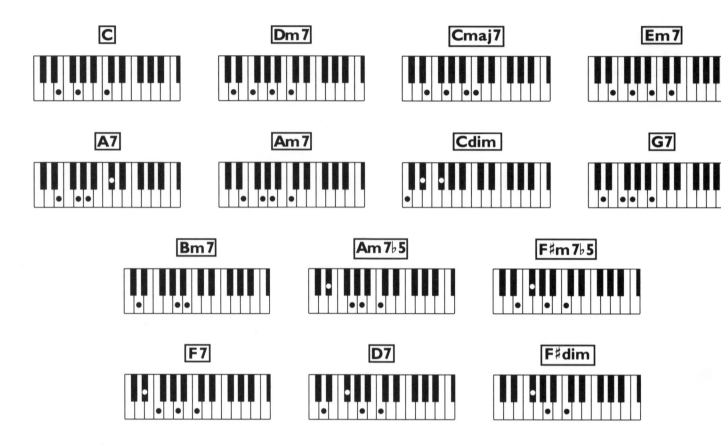

Voice: **Trumpet**

Rhythm: **16 beat**

Tempo: ♩ = 84

What's it all a-bout Al - fie?___ Is it just for the mo-ment we live? What's it

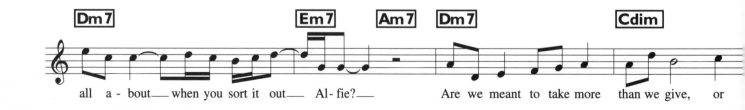

all a - bout ___ when you sort it out ___ Al - fie? ___ Are we meant to take more than we give, or

are we meant to be kind?___ And if on-ly fools are kind Al - fie,___ then I

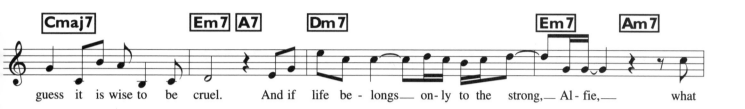

guess it is wise to be cruel. And if life be - longs___ on-ly to the strong,___ Al - fie,___ what

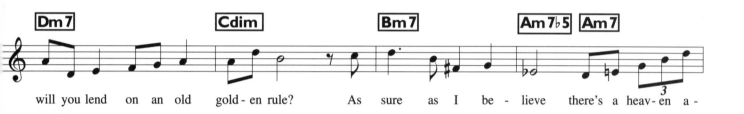

will you lend on an old gold-en rule? As sure as I be - lieve there's a heav-en a -

- bove, Al - fie. I know there's some-thing much more, some-thing ev-en non-be-liev-ers

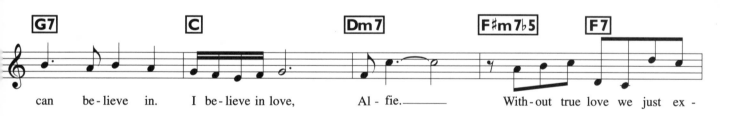

can be-lieve in. I be-lieve in love, Al - fie.___ With-out true love we just ex -

-ist, Al- fie. Un-til you find the love you've missed you're no-thing, Al - fie. When you walk let your heart

lead the way, and you'll find love a - ny day, Al - fie, Al - fie.

BEAUTY AND THE BEAST

Words by Howard Ashman
Music by Alan Menken

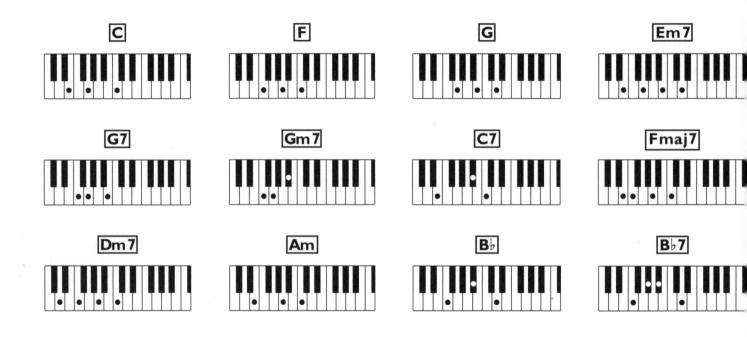

Voice: **Flute**

Rhythm: **16 beat**

Tempo: ♩ = 88

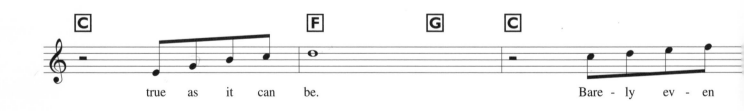

Tale as old as time,

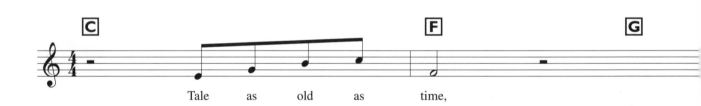

true as it can be.   Bare - ly ev - en

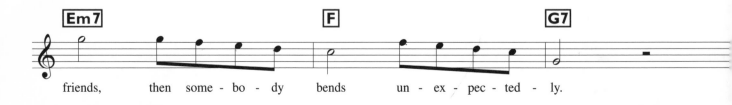

friends,   then some - bo - dy bends un - ex - pec - ted - ly.

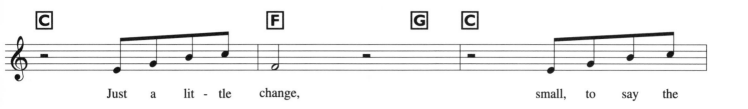

Just a lit - tle change, small, to say the

least. Both a lit - tle scared nei - ther one pre -

- pared. Beau - ty and the beast. Ev - er just the

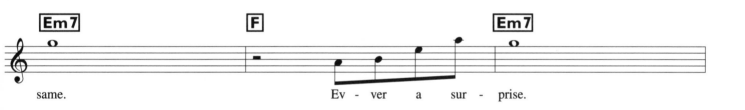

same. Ev - ver a sur - prise.

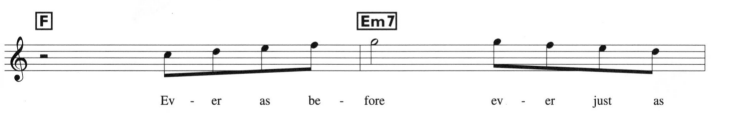

Ev - er as be - fore ev - er just as

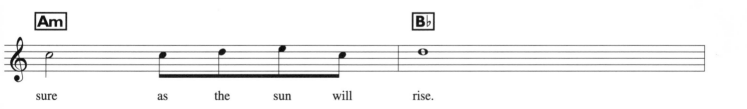

sure as the sun will rise.

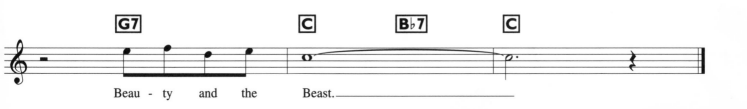

Beau - ty and the Beast._____

BLUE VELVET

Words & Music by Bernie Wayne & Lee Morris

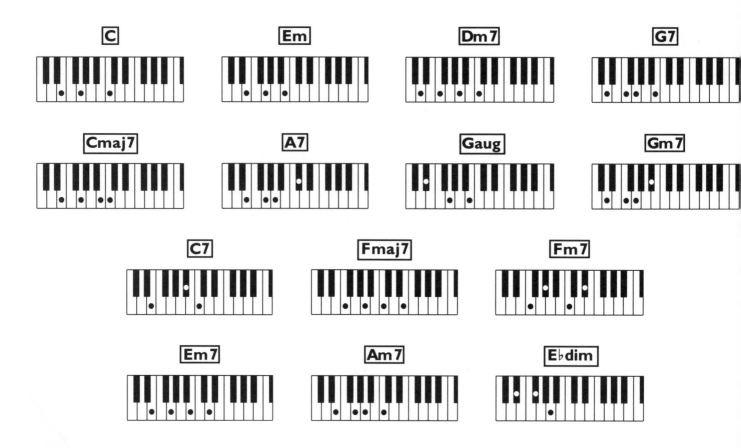

Voice: **Trumpet**

Rhythm: **2 beat**

Tempo: ♩ = 92

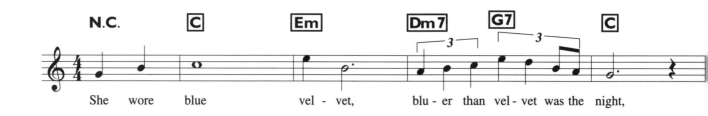

She wore blue vel - vet, blu - er than vel - vet was the night,

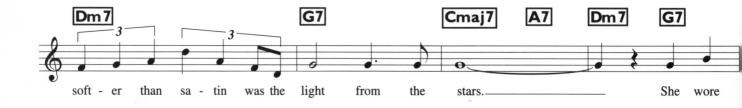

soft - er than sa - tin was the light from the stars. _____ She wore

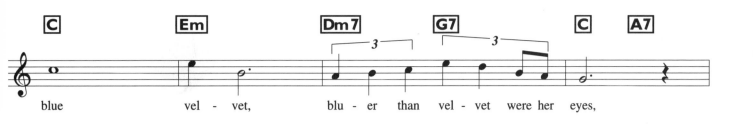

blue   vel - vet,   blu - er than   vel - vet   were her   eyes,

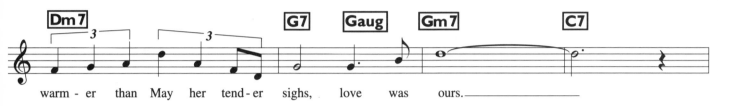

warm - er than May her tend - er sighs, love was ours.___

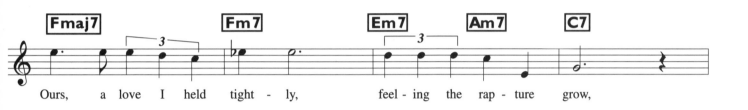

Ours,   a love I held tight - ly,   feel - ing the rap - ture grow,

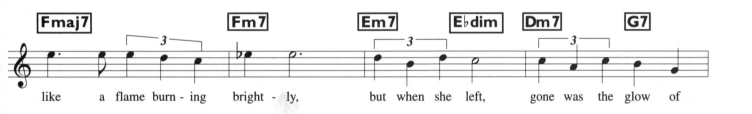

like   a flame burn - ing   bright - ly,   but when she left,   gone was the glow of

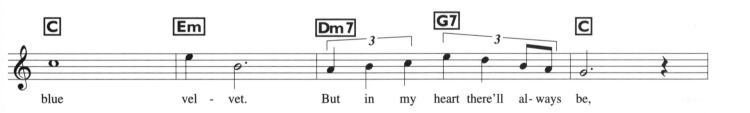

blue   vel - vet.   But   in   my   heart there'll al - ways be,

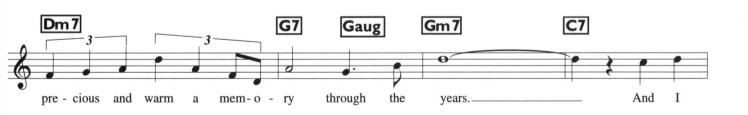

pre - cious and warm a mem - o - ry through the years.___   And I

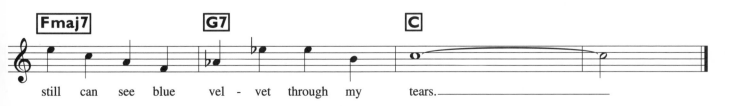

still can see blue vel - vet through my   tears.___

CIRCLE OF LIFE
(From Walt Disney Pictures' "The Lion King")
as performed by Elton John

Music by Elton John. Lyrics by Tim Rice
© Copyright 1994 Wonderland Music Company Incorporated.
Administered in the UK by Campbell Connelly & Company Limited, 8/9 Frith Street, London W1.
All Rights Reserved. International Copyright Secured.

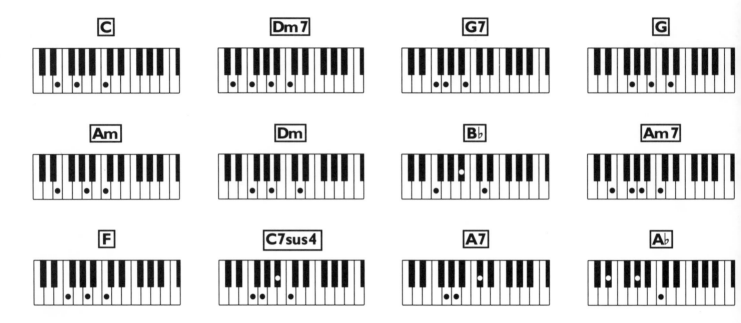

Voice:	**Saxophone**
Rhythm:	**16 beat**
Tempo:	♩ = 92

From the day we ar-rive on the pla-net and blink-ing, step in - to the sun,

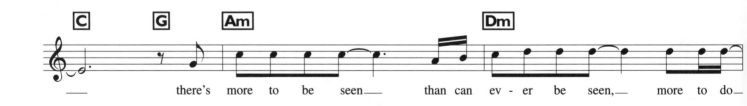

— there's more to be seen— than can ev-er be seen,— more to do—

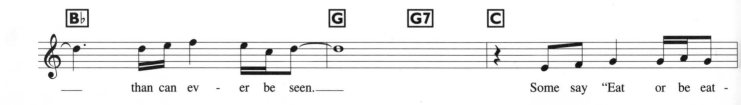

— than can ev - er be seen.— Some say "Eat or be eat -

Some say_____ "Live and let live."_____ But

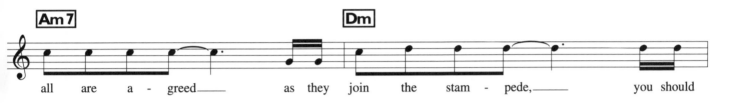

all are a - greed_____ as they join the stam - pede,_____ you should

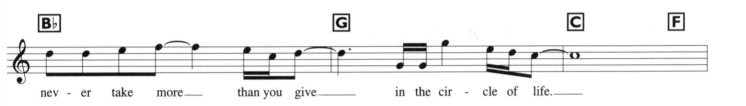

nev - er take more_____ than you give_____ in the cir - cle of life._____

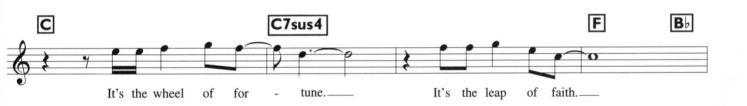

It's the wheel of for - tune._____ It's the leap of faith._____

It's the band of___ hope,_____ 'til we find our___ place_____

on the path un - wind - ing_____ in the cir - cle,_____

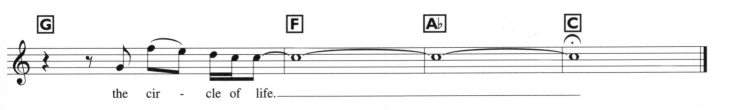

the cir - cle of life._____

LOVE IS A SONG

Words by Larry Morey
Music by Frank Churchill

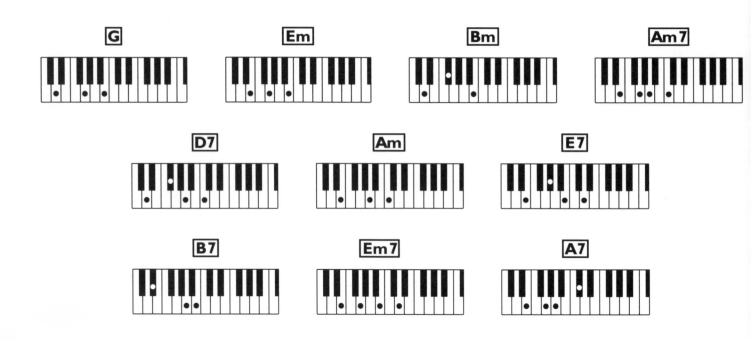

Voice: **Clarinet**

Rhythm: **Ballad**

Tempo: ♩ = 104

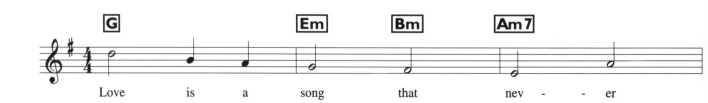

Love is a song that nev - - er

ends.   Life   may - be   swift   and

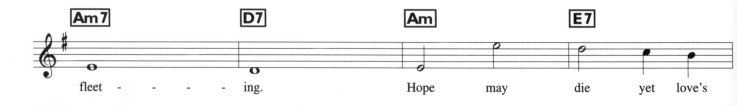

fleet - - - ing.   Hope   may   die   yet   love's

LOVE IS ALL AROUND

Words & Music by Reg Presley

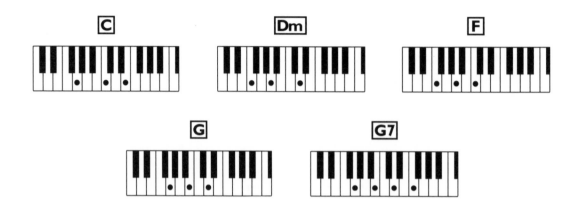

Voice: **Saxophone**

Rhythm: **Ballad**

Tempo: ♩ = 84

I feel it in my fing-ers, I feel it in my toes.—

— The love that's all a-round me,

and so the feel-ing grows.— It's writ-ten on the wind,

it's ev-'ry-where I go.—— So if you real-ly love me,

LOVER

Music by Richard Rodgers
Words by Lorenz Hart

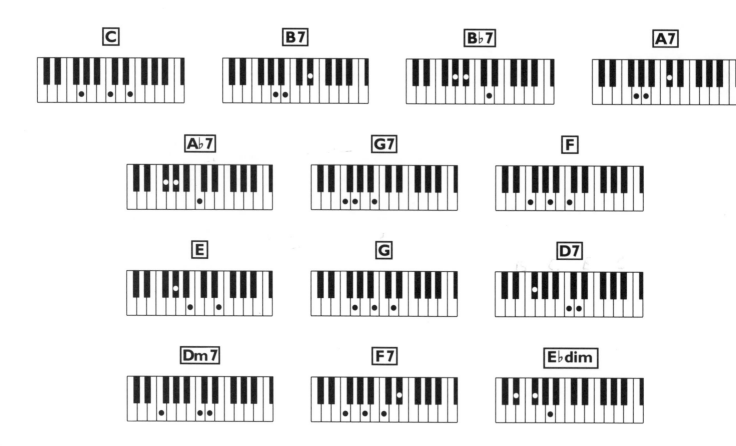

Voice:	**Trumpet**
Rhythm:	**Jazz waltz**
Tempo:	♩ = 126

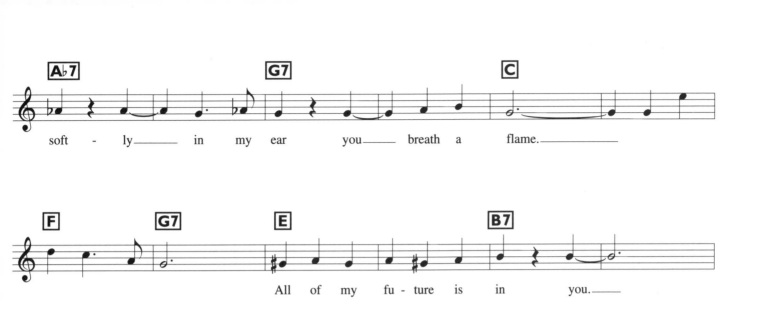

soft - ly in my ear you breath a flame.

All of my fu - ture is in you.

Your ev - 'ry plan I de - sign. Pro - mise you'll al - ways con -

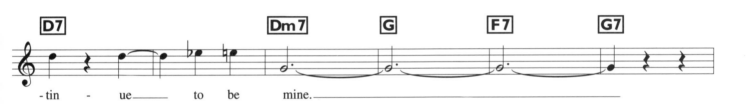

-tin - ue to be mine.

Lov - er, please be ten - der, when you're ten - der fears de -

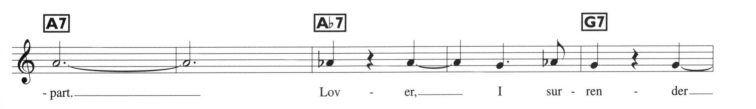

- part. Lov - er, I sur - ren - der

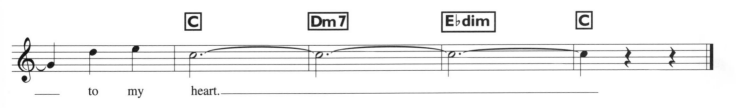

to my heart.

MONA LISA

Words & Music by Jay Livingston & Ray Evans
© Copyright 1949 Famous Music Corporation, USA.
All Rights Reserved. International Copyright Secured.

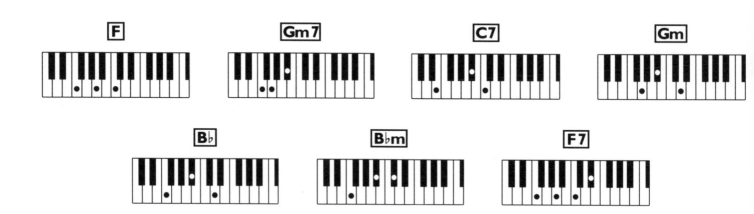

Voice: **Clarinet**

Rhythm: **Ballad**

Tempo: ♩ = 92

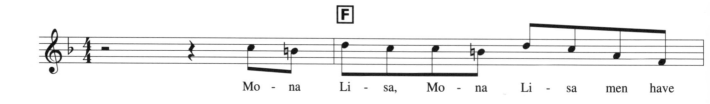

Mo - na Li - sa, Mo - na Li - sa men have

named you. You're so like the la - dy with the mys - tic

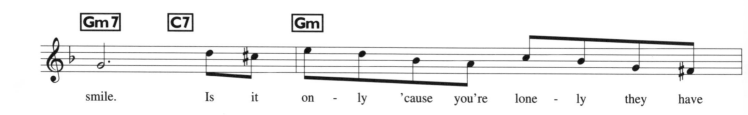

smile. Is it on - ly 'cause you're lone - ly they have

blamed you for that Mo - na Li - sa strange - ness in your

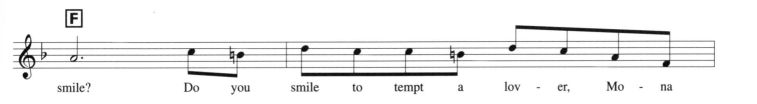

F

smile? Do you smile to tempt a lov - er, Mo - na

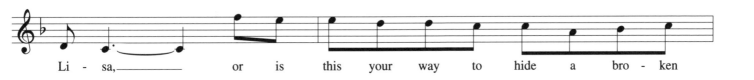

Li - sa,————— or is this your way to hide a bro - ken

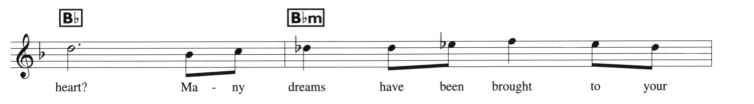

Bb   Bbm

heart? Ma - ny dreams have been brought to your

F   C7

door - step. They just lie there, and they

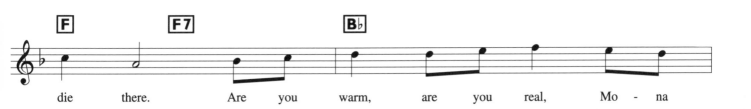

F   F7   Bb

die there. Are you warm, are you real, Mo - na

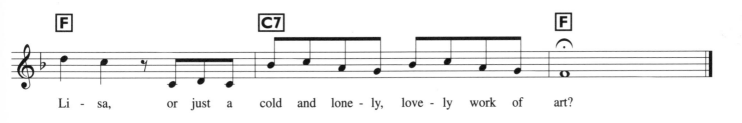

F   C7   F

Li - sa, or just a cold and lone - ly, love - ly work of art?

MOON RIVER

Music by Henry Mancini
Words by Johnny Mercer

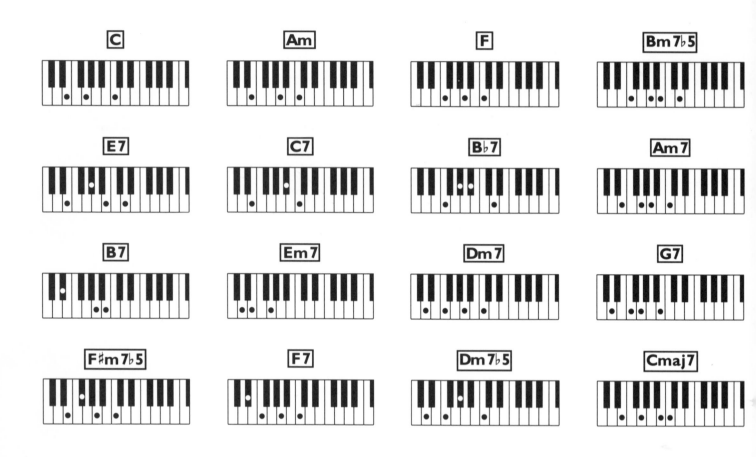

Voice: **Saxophone** 14 1

Rhythm: **Jazz waltz** 72

Tempo: ♩ = 96

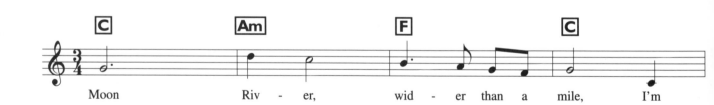

Moon Riv - er, wid - er than a mile, I'm

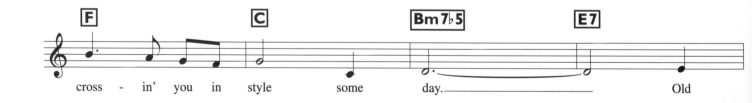

cross - in' you in style some day. Old

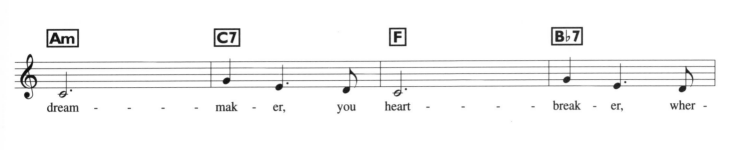

dream - - - - mak - er, you heart - - - - break - er, wher -

- ev - er you're go - in', ___ I'm go - in' ___ your way.

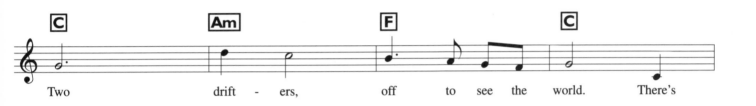

Two drift - ers, off to see the world. There's

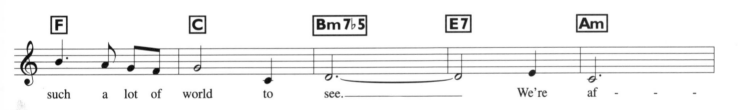

such a lot of world to see. ___ We're af - - -

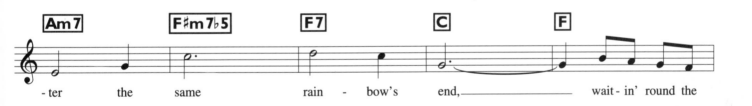

- ter the same rain - bow's end, ___ wait - in' round the

bend, ___ my Huck - le - ber - ry friend, Moon

Riv - er ___ and me. ___

MOONLIGHT BECOMES YOU

Music by Jimmy Van Heusen
Words by Johnny Burke

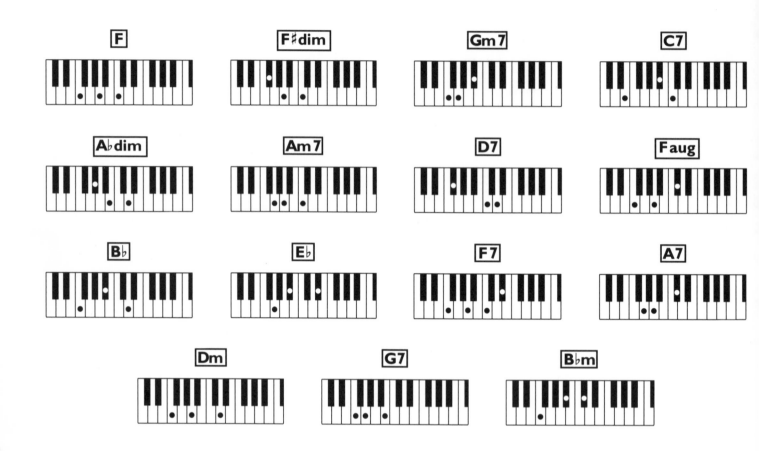

Voice: **Saxophone**

Rhythm: **Ballad**

Tempo: ♩ = 88

Moon - light be - comes you, it goes with your

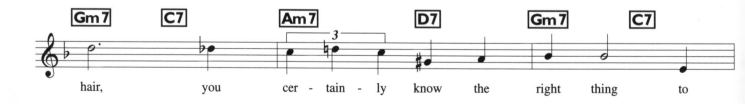

hair, you cer - tain - ly know the right thing to

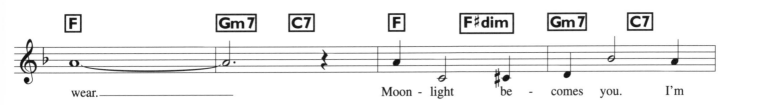
wear._____ Moon - light be - comes you. I'm

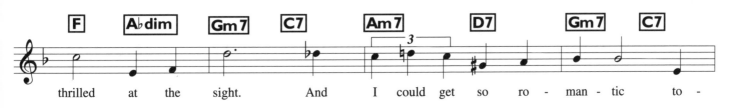
thrilled at the sight. And I could get so ro - man - tic to -

- night._____ You're all dressed up to go dream - ing, now

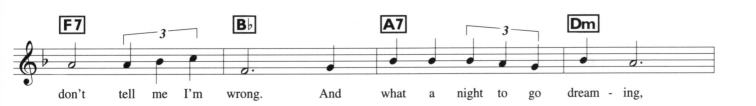
don't tell me I'm wrong. And what a night to go dream - ing,

mind if I tag a - long? If I say I love you, I

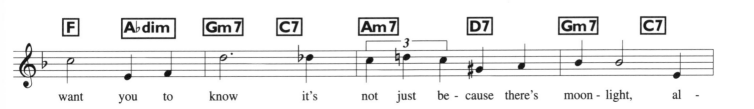
want you to know it's not just be - cause there's moon - light, al -

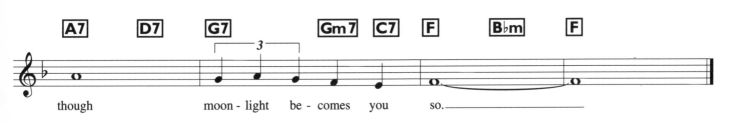
though moon - light be - comes you so._____

MRS ROBINSON

Words & Music by Paul Simon

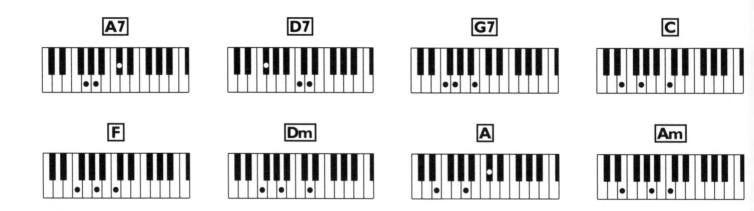

Voice: **Accordion**

Rhythm: **Soft rock**

Tempo: ♩ = 112

We'd like to know a lit - tle bit___ a - bout___

you for our files._____ We'd like to help you

learn to help your - self._____ Look a - round you, all___

___ you see___ are sym - pa - the - tic eyes._____

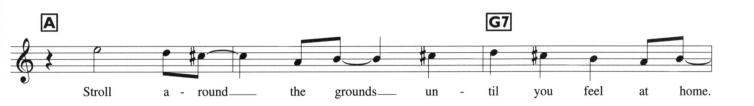

Stroll a - round the grounds un - til you feel at home.

And here's to you Mrs Rob - in - son,

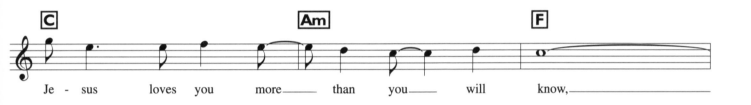

Je - sus loves you more than you will know,

(wo wo wo.) God bless you

please Mrs Rob - in - son, hea - ven holds a place

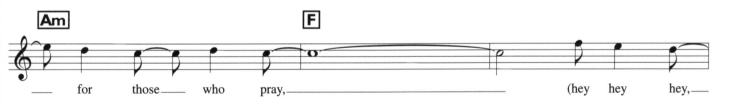

for those who pray, (hey hey hey,

hey hey hey.)

MY KIND OF TOWN (CHICAGO IS)

Words by Sammy Cahn
Music by Jimmy Van Heusen

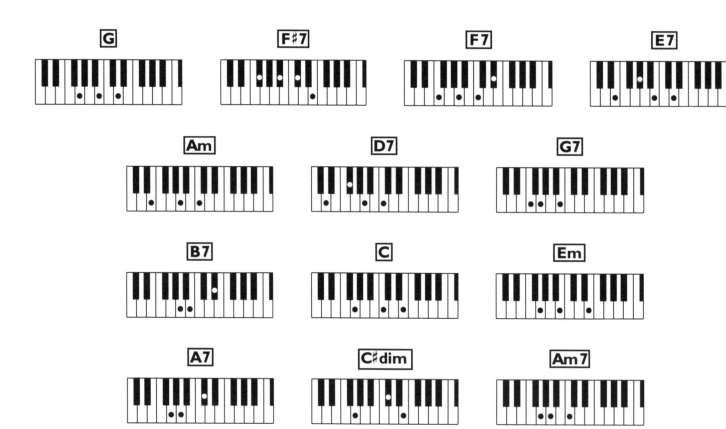

Voice: **Clarinet**

Rhythm: **2 beat**

Tempo: ♩ = 144

It's   my   kind   of

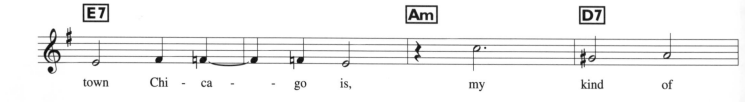

town   Chi - ca - go   is,   my   kind   of

town Chi - ca - - go is. My kind of

peo - ple too,_____ peo - ple who_____

smile at you and each time I

roam, Chi - ca - - go is call - - ing me

home. Chi - ca - - go is one town that

won't let you down,_____ it's my_____ kind

of town._____

SPEAK SOFTLY LOVE

Music by Nino Rota
Words by Larry Kusik

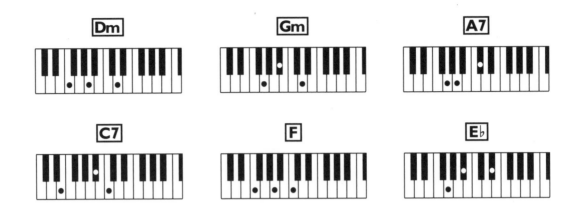

Voice: **Clarinet**

Rhythm: **Ballad**

Tempo: ♩ = 88

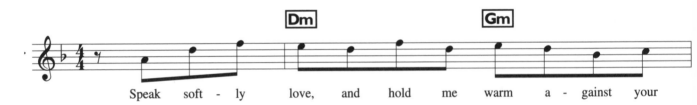

Speak soft - ly love, and hold me warm a - gainst your

heart. I feel your words, the ten - der trem - bling mo - ments

start. We're in a world our ve - ry

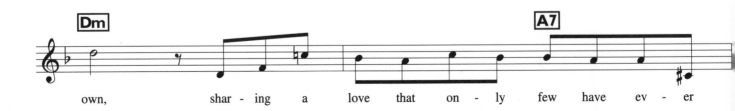

own, shar - ing a love that on - ly few have ev - er

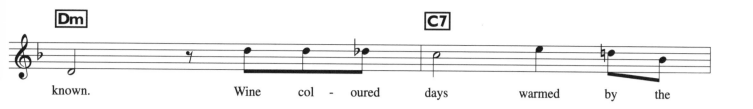

known.   Wine   col - oured   days   warmed   by   the

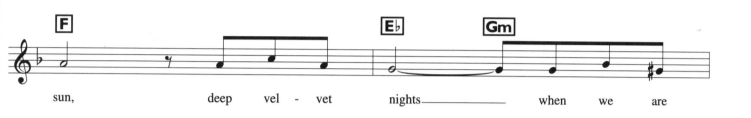

sun,   deep   vel - vet   nights_____   when   we   are

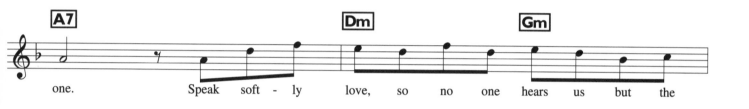

one.   Speak   soft - ly   love,   so   no   one   hears   us   but   the

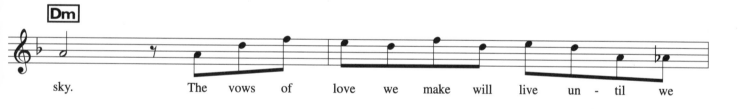

sky.   The   vows   of   love   we   make   will   live   un - til   we

die.   My   life   is   yours_____   and   all   be -

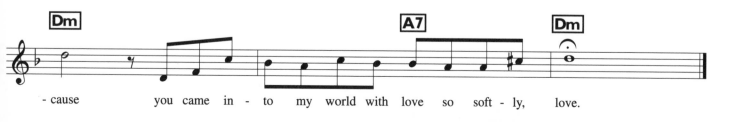

- cause   you   came   in - to   my   world   with   love   so   soft - ly,   love.

STELLA BY STARLIGHT

Music by Victor Young
Words by Ned Washington

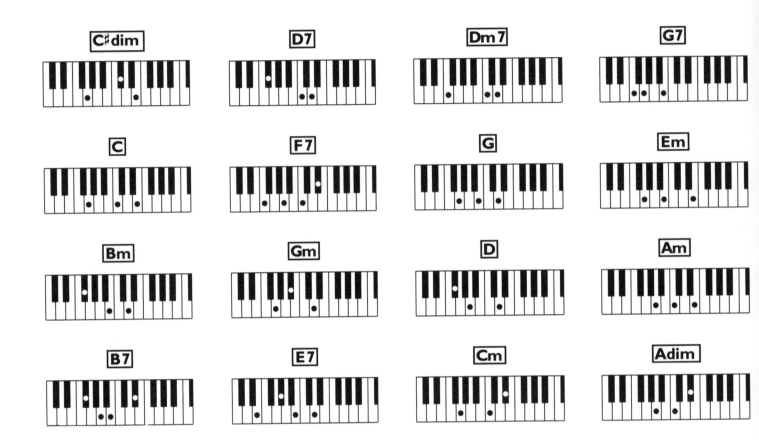

Voice: **Trumpet**

Rhythm: **Beguine**

Tempo: ♩ = 116

C#dim The song____ a ro - bin sings____ D7 through

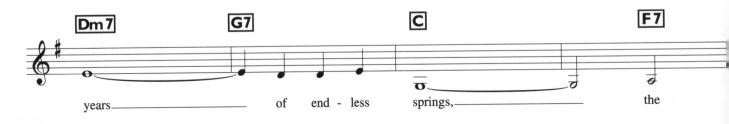

Dm7 years____ G7 of end - less C springs, F7 the

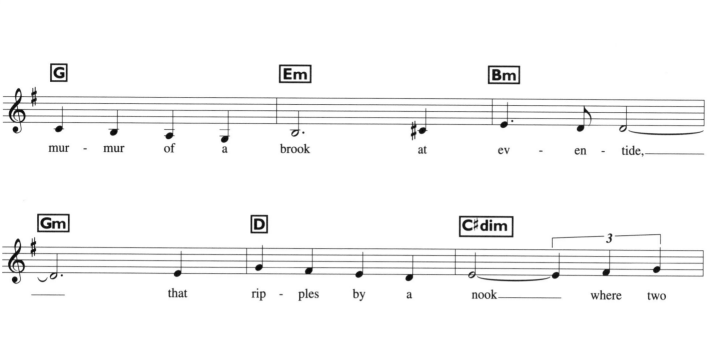

mur - mur of a brook at ev - en - tide,____ that rip - ples by a nook____ where two

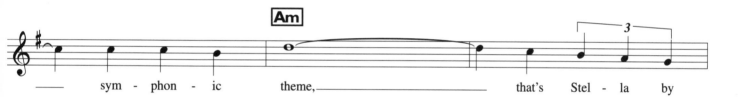

lov - ers hide,____ a great____ sym - phon - ic theme,____ that's Stel - la by

star - light,____ and not a dream.____ She's

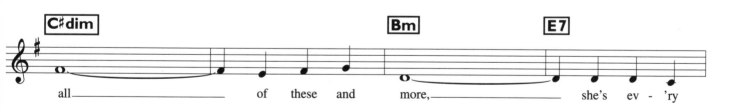

all____ of these and more,____ she's ev - 'ry

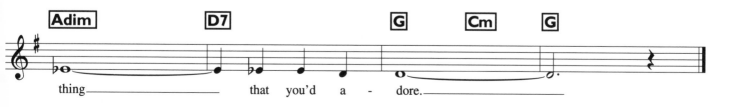

thing____ that you'd a - dore.____

STRANGERS IN THE NIGHT

Words by Charles Singleton & Eddie Snyder
Music by Bert Kaempfert

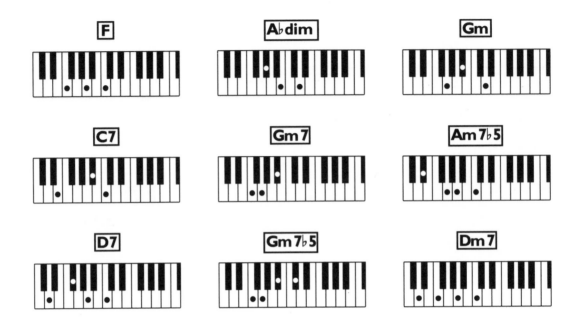

Voice: **Piano**

Rhythm: **Beguine**

Tempo: ♩ = 100

Strang-ers in the night___ ex-chang-ing glan-ces, wond-'ring in the night___

___ what were the chan-ces we'd be shar-ing love___ be-fore the night was

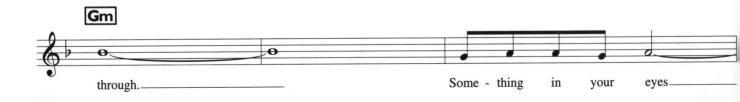

through.___ Some-thing in your eyes___

was so in-vit-ing, some-thing in your smile___ was so ex-cit-ing,

some-thing in my heart___ told me I must have you.___

Strang-ers in the night,___ two lone-ly peo-ple we were strang-ers in the night,___

___ up to the mo-ment when we said our first hel-lo, lit-tle did we know

love was just a glance a-way, a warm em-brac-ing dance a-way. And ev-er since that night___

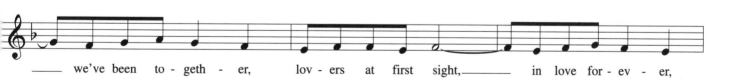
___ we've been to-geth-er, lov-ers at first sight,___ in love for-ev-er,

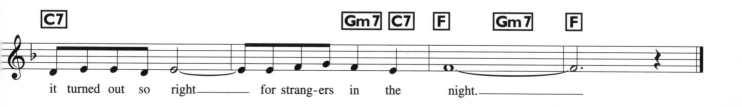
it turned out so right___ for strang-ers in the night.___

TAKE MY BREATH AWAY

Words by Tom Whitlock
Music by Giorgio Moroder
© Copyright 1986 Giorgio Moroder Publishing Company & Famous Music Corporation, USA.
All Rights Reserved. International Copyright Secured.

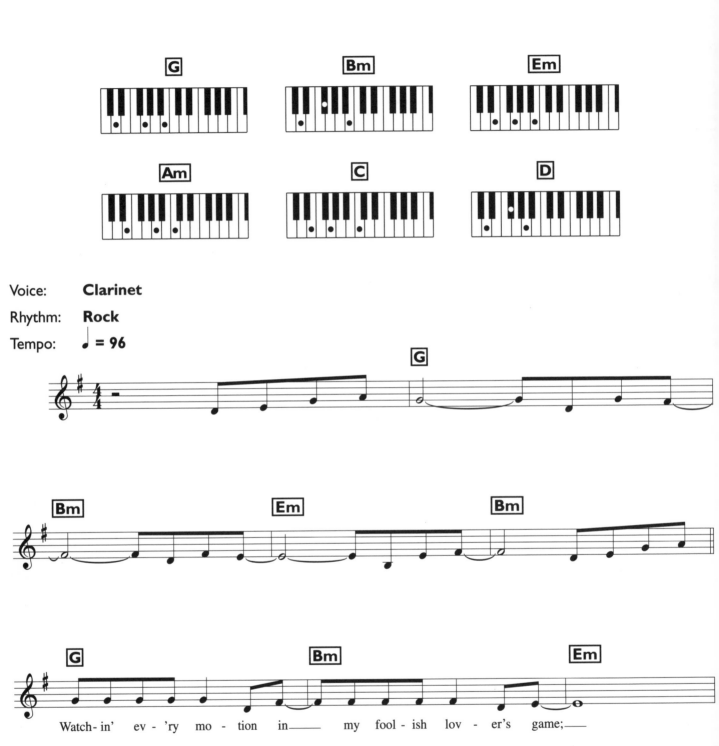

Voice: **Clarinet**

Rhythm: **Rock**

Tempo: ♩ = 96

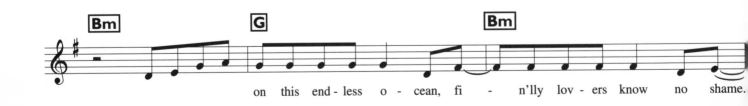

Watch-in' ev-'ry mo-tion in___ my fool-ish lov-er's game;___

on this end-less o-cean, fi - n'lly lov-ers know no shame.

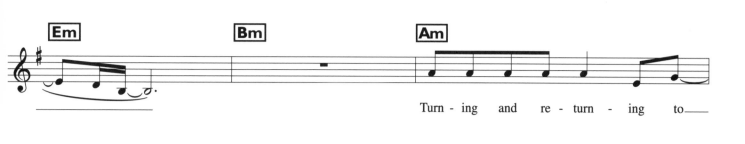

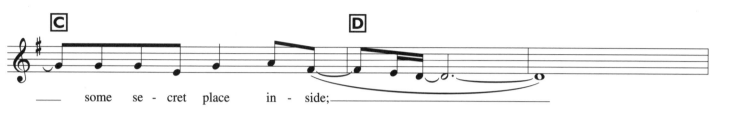

some se - cret place in - side;

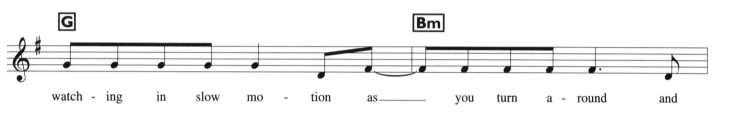

watch - ing in slow mo - tion as you turn a - round and

say, "Take my breath a - way."

My love, "Take my breath a -

- way."

Repeat to fade

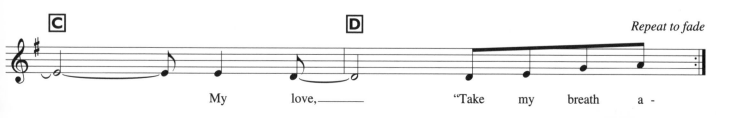

My love, "Take my breath a -

THANKS FOR THE MEMORY

Words & Music by Leo Robin & Ralph Rainger
© Copyright 1937 Famous Music Corporation, USA.
All Rights Reserved. International Copyright Secured.

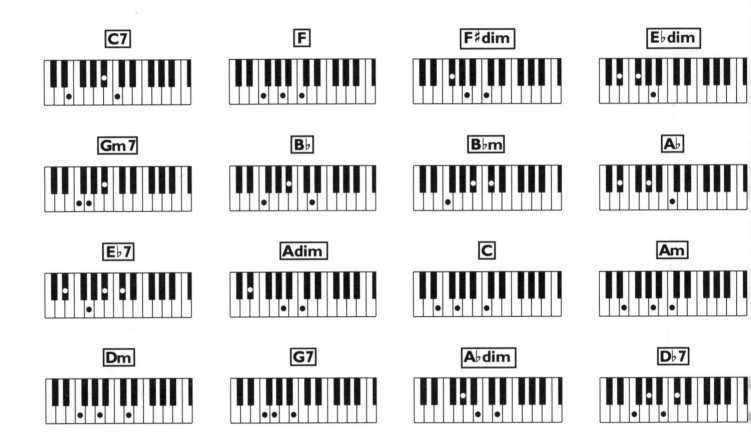

Voice: **Trumpet**

Rhythm: **2 beat**

Tempo: ♩ = 92

Thanks for the mem - o - ry of can - dle - light and wine, ___

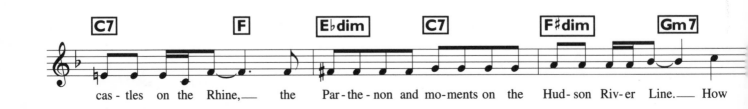

cas - tles on the Rhine, ___ the Par - the - non and mo - ments on the Hud - son Riv - er Line. ___ How

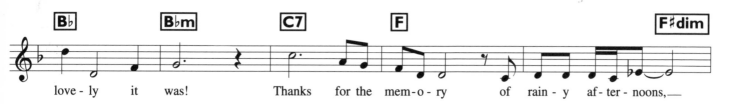

love - ly it was! Thanks for the mem-o-ry of rain-y af-ter-noons,—

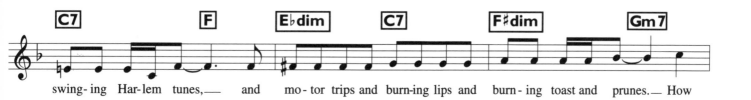

swing-ing Har-lem tunes,— and mo-tor trips and burn-ing lips and burn-ing toast and prunes.— How

love - ly it was! We said good-bye with a high-ball; then

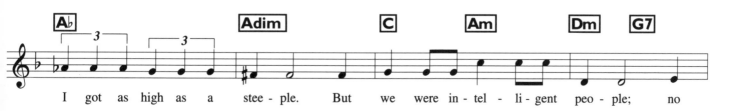

I got as high as a stee-ple. But we were in-tel-li-gent peo-ple; no

tears, no fuss, hur-ray for us. So thanks for the mem-o-ry and strict-ly en-tre-nous,

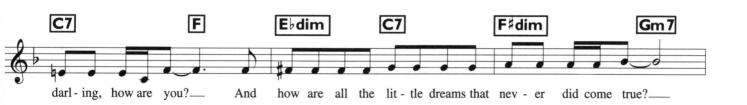

darl-ing, how are you?— And how are all the lit-tle dreams that nev-er did come true?—

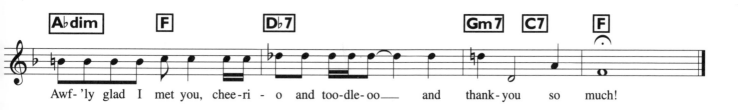

Awf-'ly glad I met you, chee-ri-o and too-dle-oo— and thank-you so much!

THAT'S AMORÉ

Words & Music by Jack Brooks & Harry Warren

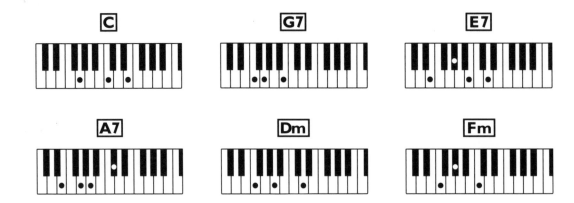

Voice: **Accordion**

Rhythm: **Waltz**

Tempo: ♩ = 138

When the moon hits your eye like a big piz-za pie, that's a-

-mor-é_____ When the world seems to shine like you've had to much

wine, that's a-mor-é._____ Bells will ring, ting-a-ling-a-

-ling, ting-a-ling-a-ling, and you'll sing, "Vee-ta bel-la."_____

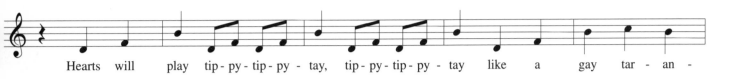
Hearts will play tip-py-tip-py-tay, tip-py-tip-py-tay like a gay tar-an-

C
-tel - la._____ When the stars make you drool just like

G7
pas - ta fa - zool, that's a - mor - é._____ When you

E7
dance down the street with a cloud at your feet, you're in love._____

A7   **Dm**
_____ When you walk in a dream but you know you're not dream-ing, sig -

C   **G7**
- nor - - é._____ Scuz - za me, but you see, back in

C   **Fm**   **C**
old Na - po - li, that's a - mor - é._____

TRY A LITTLE TENDERNESS

Words & Music by Harry Woods, Jimmy Campbell & Reg Connelly

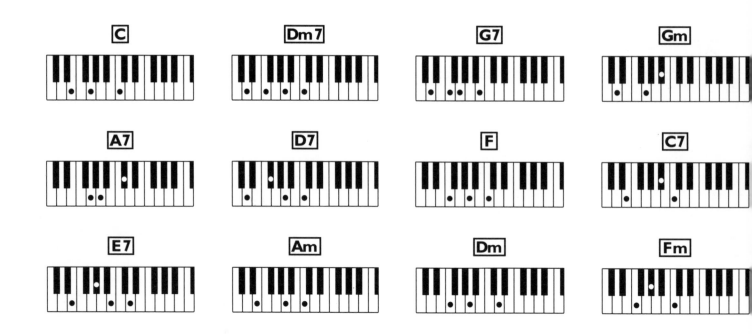

Voice: **Clarinet**

Rhythm: **2 beat**

Tempo: ♩ = 96

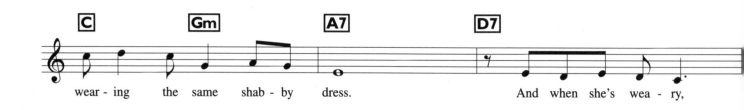

She may be wea - ry, wo - men do get wea - ry,

wear - ing the same shab - by dress. And when she's wea - ry,

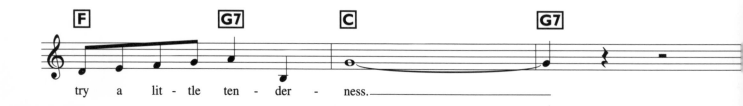

try a lit - tle ten - der - ness.

You know she's wait - ing,   just an - ti - ci - pat - ing   things she may ne - ver pos -

- sess.   While she's with - out them   try a lit - tle ten - der -

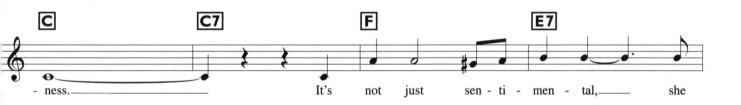

- ness.   It's not just sen - ti - men - tal,   she

has her grief and care,   and a word that's soft and

gen - tle makes it ea - si - er to bear.   You won't re - gret it,

wo - men don't for - get it,   love is their whole hap - pi - ness.

It's all so ea - sy,   try a lit - tle ten - der - ness.

UNCHAINED MELODY

Words by Hy Zaret
Music by Alex North

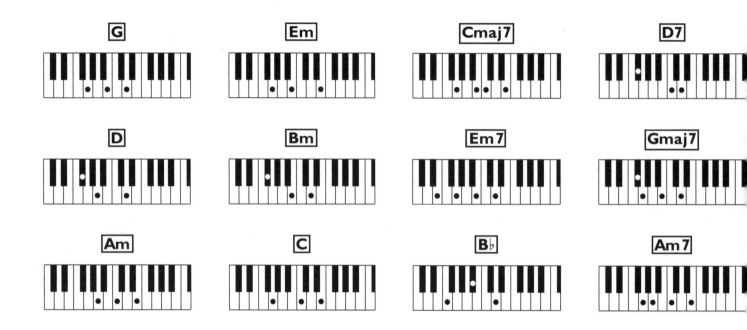

Voice: **Trumpet**

Rhythm: **Ballad**

Tempo: ♩ = 96

Oh   my   love   my   dar - ling,   I've   hun - gered   for   your

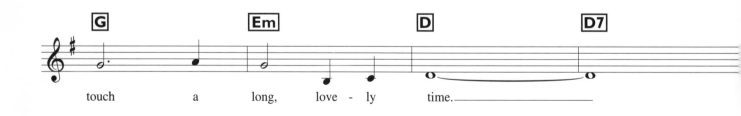

touch   a   long,   love - ly   time. _____

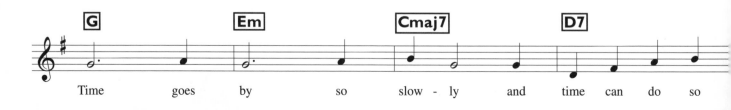

Time   goes   by   so   slow - ly   and   time   can   do   so

UP WHERE WE BELONG

Words & Music by Jack Nitzsche, Will Jennings & Buffy Sainte Marie

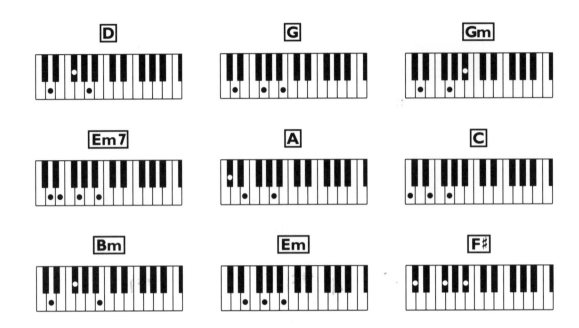

Voice: **Saxophone**

Rhythm: **16 beat**

Tempo: ♩ = 84

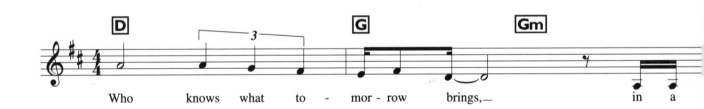

Who knows what to - mor - row brings, — in a

world few hearts sur - vive? All I know_____ is the

way I feel, — when it's real I keep it a - live. — The

EASIEST KEYBOARD COLLECTION

Easy-to-play melody line arrangements for all keyboards with chord symbols and lyrics. Suggested registration, rhythm and tempo are included for each song together with keyboard diagrams showing left-hand chord voicings used.

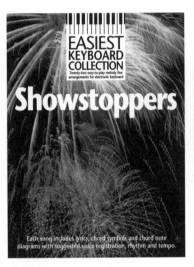 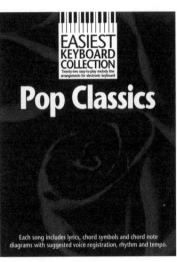 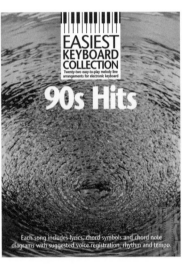 

Showstoppers
Consider Yourself (Oliver!), Do You Hear The People Sing? (Les Misérables), I Know Him So Well (Chess), Maria (West Side Story), Smoke Gets In Your Eyes (Roberta) and 17 more big stage hits.
Order No. AM944218

Pop Classics
A Whiter Shade Of Pale (Procol Harum), Bridge Over Troubled Water (Simon & Garfunkel), Crocodile Rock (Elton John) and nineteen more classic pop hits, including Hey Jude (The Beatles), Imagine (John Lennon), Massachusetts (The Bee Gees) and Stars (Simply Red).
Order No. AM944196

90s Hits
Over twenty of the greatest hits of the 1990s, including Always (Bon Jovi), Fields Of Gold (Sting), Have I Told You Lately (Rod Stewart), One Sweet Day (Mariah Carey), Say You'll Be There (Spice Girls), and Wonderwall (Oasis).
Order No. AM944229

TV Themes
Twenty-two great theme from popular TV series, including Casualty, EastEnders, Gladiators, Heartbeat, I'm Always He (Baywatch), Red Dwarf a The Black Adder.
Order No. AM944207

Also available...

Film Themes, Order No. AM952050   **Chart Hits**, Order No. AM952083
Jazz Classics, Order No. AM952061   **Classical Themes**, Order No. AM952094
Classic Blues, Order No. AM950697   **Christmas**, Order No. AM952105
Love Songs, Order No. AM950708   **Ballads**, Order No. AM952116
Pop Hits, Order No. AM952072   **Broadway**, Order No. AM952127